Starting a Business in Australia: A Practical Guide

BY

ROMEO CAPORASO

TABLE OF CONTENTS

BIOGRAPHY OF ROMEO CAPORASO

Romeo Caporaso was born and raised in Adelaide to Italian migrant parents. Finishing school at 16 and university at 19 taught him the value of discipline and early goal setting, qualities that sit at the heart of every successful business venture. After completing university in 1992, he began his career in Business Banking at Commonwealth Bank, working in Adelaide and Sydney's Eastern suburbs. His time in banking gave him firsthand experience in how businesses are funded, managed, and evaluated. At just 23, he purchased his first property in Hurstville, a milestone that shaped his long-term interest in financial planning and wealth building.

When Romeo returned to Adelaide, he continued strengthening his understanding of finance and compliance through accounting roles at RAA Insurance and Rossdale Homes. Implementing the newly introduced Goods and Services Tax (GST) during this period gave him practical insight into the exact tax concepts he now teaches new business owners. He later worked for the Australian Taxation Office, where he gained a deep understanding of tax law, reporting requirements, and the common mistakes people make when starting a business — insights that directly inform the guidance in this book.

Romeo eventually transitioned from employment to self-employment, starting businesses in personal training, bookkeeping, and website services. These early ventures taught him the challenges new entrepreneurs face, including irregular income, marketing struggles, and learning how to manage every role in a business. In 2010, he reached his long-held goal of becoming a tax agent and began building his accounting practice from the ground up. Starting with no clients, no staff, and a home office, he grew his firm into a Xero-certified and later Xero Gold Partner practice, issuing over $5 million in invoices and supporting a large base of business clients. His adoption of online accounting systems in 2013 made him an early leader in digital, cloud-based bookkeeping — a core part of the advice found in *The Startup Guide*.

Across his career, Romeo has helped hundreds of new and established businesses understand tax obligations, choose the right structure, manage cash flow, stay compliant, and build long-term financial health. He has also launched dozens of accountants into their careers through training and internships. His shift from traditional MYOB bookkeeping in 2005 to a paperless, technology-driven system reflects the exact transition he now encourages for new business owners who want efficient, modern reporting.

Romeo's experience extends beyond business accounting. He has overseen the setup of more than one hundred Self-Managed Super Funds (SMSFs) and actively promotes wealth creation as part of responsible business ownership. His own SMSF holds both property and shares, including a property purchased outright with no loan — demonstrating the long-term benefits of disciplined financial planning. His property development journey, which includes transforming his parents' home into townhouses, strengthened his understanding of tax, construction businesses, and investment strategy. These real-world experiences help him teach new business owners how to think beyond day-to-day operations and plan for growth and financial security.

Romeo practices what he teaches. His story mirrors the journey of many new business owners — starting small, learning through challenges, and growing with the right systems and guidance. His background in tax, compliance, financial investing, marketing, and modern accounting technology forms the foundation of this book. *The Startup Guide* brings together the knowledge he has gained across three decades to help Australians start and build a business with confidence, clarity, and the right tools.

Meet Romeo by calling 08 8337 4460 for a coffee and chat. Learn more about Tax Accounting Adelaide and schedule your business planning and tax minimisation session.

Book in for your business advice session at https://bit.ly/4r95k4P. More information at New business advice Adelaide | Tax Accounting Adelaide or https://bit.ly/4i8jOxH.

NEW BUSINESS ADVICE IN AUSTRALIA

INTRODUCTION

Starting a business in Australia is an exciting yet challenging journey. Success depends on careful planning, understanding financial and legal obligations, and tracking your business performance.

It is an exciting time to set sail. Set new goals such as earning more than your previous job, improving the delivery of a good or service, and perhaps working less with greater reward and satisfaction. With the right efforts, your business can return greater remuneration and even give business equity worth that may be sellable down the track. This potential sale of your business, the freedom of setting your work hours and practices and the reward if you get it right, that will be harvested for you rather than someone else, your employer. Undoubtedly, initially, the importance of self-belief and goal setting is of huge importance. Without purpose, you may not get anywhere. Setting goals and sales budgets can increase your chances of success enormously. A common first goal is to earn more than your previous job or business. I call this the old job break-even point. I have also seen many people transition into business by staying with some part-time employment while they commence their business, which gives them a level of stability to get the business the ground or see if it can indeed thrive.

Being self-employed requires a different mindset from being an employee. Being self-employed may mean you cannot switch off and leave your work behind 9 to 5, or take a holiday from it as easily. It may be more relentless and tiring. It may mean you cannot expect to draw stable wages immediately, or they may be inconsistent. You may need to develop various new and diverse skills as a business owner while learn the art of being an effective business owner. These skills may include improving technical offering, delegating and outsourcing, managing your business numbers, improving your sales and marketing skills, and the fine art of recruiting and keeping staff, to name a few.

Key Points:

- **Know your Numbers:** Monitor cash flow, expenses, revenue, and profitability to make informed decisions. Without understanding your scoreboard, you may feel lost and overwhelmed. Simple online accounting software is recommended, especially if you are GST registered or have wages.

- **Profitability:** Ensure your business is both enjoyable and profitable, providing a good return on your time. Don't do anything just to make money; do something you are passionate about. You must maintain the discipline of keeping records and tracking the income and expenditure of your business to keep your success on track to your goals and meet tax obligations.

- **Tax Planning and compliance:** Set aside 30% of profits for tax obligations to avoid unexpected bills and ensure financial stability. You would need to report BAS returns if GST-registered and include business income and expenses in annual tax returns. You will need to issue compliant tax invoices for your goods and services.

UNDERSTANDING SOME TAX BASICS FOR INDIVIDUALS IN AUSTRALIA

Australia has a complex tax system. Here is a brief explanation of how tax returns work.

Australian tax returns for individuals will include all assessable incomes (like wages and salaries, business income, investment income) less deductions (like uniforms, business car costs, home office costs and cost of tax preparation fee), which gives you what the Australian Taxation Office (ATO) calls TAXABLE INCOME.

Once you have your taxable income, depending on how high it is, you are taxed progressively more, as shown in this table of the Income tax rates. This is called Tax on your Taxable Income.

Most income is traceable to the ATO by quoting your Tax File Number TFN or Australian Business Number ABN in business in conducting your income-producing affairs, such as business, employment and investing, such as share dividends and bank interest.

This information will prefill when you do a tax return, making it easier not to omit income that is taxable.

However, for Business income, you do need to make these income declarations yourself, as the ATO will not calculate business income or expenses for you.

Tax rates 2025-2026

The following rates for 2025-2026 apply from 1 July 2025.

Taxable income	Tax on this income
0 - $18,200	Nil
$18,201 - $45,000	16c for each $1 over $18,200
$45,001 - $135,000	$4,288 plus 30.0c for each $1 over $45,000
$135,001 - $190,000	$31,288 plus 37c for each $1 over $135,000
$190,001 and over	$51,638 plus 45c for each $1 over $180,000

The above rates **do not** include the Medicare levy of 2%.

Please check current or future tax rates at the ATO website: <u>Tax rates – Australian resident | Australian Taxation Office</u>

Once you have calculated the tax on taxable income, you add the Medicare levy, an extra tax levied. Then you take off any taxes paid (such as on business tax instalments and taxes taken out of wages) and any tax offsets (such as zone offset) to get your tax return refund or amount payable. If you have already paid more tax than the tax on taxable income, then you get a refund. If you have paid less tax than the tax on taxable income, then you need to pay the tax payable generally in March after the tax return period following the

30th of June. Australian tax return years fall in fiscal years from 1st July to 30th June.

For more examples and explanations of Income, deductions, taxes paid, and tax offsets, visit these ATO links

Income you must declare | Australian Taxation Office

Deductions you can claim | Australian Taxation Office

Tax offsets | Australian Taxation Office

BUSINESS PLANNING & ENTITY SELECTION

Choosing the Right Business Structure

The structure you choose impacts taxation, liability protection, and business flexibility. Below are the main options:

Structure	Description	Advantages	Disadvantages	Tax Treatment
Sole Trader	Operates as an individual.	Full control, low cost, simple setup. Easy to take out drawings from the business of additional funds from profits.	Unlimited liability; personal assets at risk.	Taxed on profits which accumulate as taxable income in the individuals tax returns and taxed at individual tax rates
Partnership	Two or more individuals share responsibilities	Combined skills/resources, shared costs. Easy to Take out drawings from the business of additional funds from profits. However, should be done on an	Joint liability; formal agreement needed. The exit of partners without partnership agreements can cause	All partners are Taxed on their distributed profits which accumulate as taxable income in the individual's tax returns and are taxed at individual tax rates

| | | | even basis to be equal. | troubled separations and disruption to the business. | |
| Compa ny (Pty Ltd) | Separate legal entity. | Asset protection, tax advantages. | More complex. Higher set-up and ongoing fees to ASIC and company accounting. More difficult to take out excess profits to owner individuals as this must be done by wages or dividends. May need reliance on accountants. Cost are an | Tax on all company profits is at a flat rate from 1st $of profit. This can be beneficial if the large profit as lower than other entities. Individuals associated with a company should take income in wages or dividends of at least $45000 if have no other personal income to utilise the lower tax brackets of the tax-free threshold and the next band of 16% both of which are less than the minimum company tax rate of 25%. |

			annual ASIC return fee of around $300, set up company cost around $1100. Annual tax from $880 and BAS returns from $330 per quarter.	
Trust	Trustee manages assets for beneficiaries	Tax advantages as can distribute profits to family member with the lowest tax liability. Can be held for family without transfer instead of estate planning.. Can provide asset	Can need guidance from accountants to meet tax rules with resolutions set to who shall receive distributions of trust profits.. Like a company, it can be	Amounts distributed to other entities are taxed as per those entity types. Best suited to a family business with spouse or adult children with lower income to distribute to or with a corporate owner who can also be distributed to

		protection too if the owner of the trust is a company trustee.	more difficult to establish with additional costs, especially if a trustee owner if a company	

Guidance on which accounting entity type is commonly advised by tax agents, who can factor in all your circumstances to determine the best entity type for your situation.

Applying for an Australian Business Number (ABN)

An ABN is essential for legally operating a business in Australia. Steps include:

1. **Decide Business Structure:** Consult a tax advisor for tailored advice.

2. **Submit Online Application:** Use the Australian Business Register. There is currently no cost from this government agency. If there is a fee, you are most likely using an ABN service provider. https://abr.gov.au/For-Business,-Super-funds---Charities/Applying-for-an-ABN/

3. **Provide Business Details:** Include trading name, operations, and identity verification.

4. **Receive ABN:** Enables GST registration, tax credits, and invoicing. These may be issued immediately or within the ATO service standard time of 28 days.

5. **Get new business advice specific to your circumstances**

We recommend seeking an accountant's advice to advise you on which accounting structure best suits your new business venture and registering for your ABN. Book your new business advice session here.

LEGAL & COMPLIANCE ESSENTIALS

Business Name Registration

To legally operate with a business name that is not your birth name, businesses must:

- Register their business name with ASIC. Register a business name | ASIC

- Obtain industry-specific licenses or permits (e.g., health permits for food services). Australian Business Licence and Information Service - ABLIS

- Comply with workplace laws when hiring employees (Fair Work Act). Welcome to the Fair Work Ombudsman website

- Register for worker's insurance in your state. Here is South Australia's ReturnToWorkSA online services

Key Tax Compliance

Key tax obligations include:

- **Annual Tax return reporting:** In accordance with Australian tax laws, each business structure will need to declare income and expenses of its business operations in the relevant tax years, which end 30 June. Lodgement deadlines vary from 31 October for self-lodgers to 15 May for taxpayers with a tax agent... It is vital to lodge these on time to avoid fines and late payment interest charges. Getting behind on tax obligations in business can really get you into a big debt trap, so keep up to date with income tax returns.

- **PAYG Tax Instalments:** This is a way to prepay tax on business income. Think of Pay As You Go tax (PAYG) instalments as something equivalent to having tax taken out of your wage pay check, and that is mostly taking care of the tax paid for your yearly tax return. The tax return is a reconciliation for the tax paid during the year, as being overpaid, a refund or underpaid, tax payable. So, when you are a business owner, this is an ATO-created system of prepaying tax towards your next tax return. This is meant to smooth out your tax-paying process by paying quarterly tax estimated on your last profit tax declarations instead of paying a large once-only tax payment at the tax return time. But when you have not yet shown a business profit yet such as in the first year, no PAYG instalment is raised, hence you need to provision for your tax until PAYG instalments commence. Even then, they are only an estimate, and the actual tax payable may vary if profit has changed. To illustrate, we will use an example with Bob, who has a business. In his first year, he made $60k profit. He listened to my advice, and kept aside 30% of the profit which is $18k. When he did his tax return, and with deductions his actual tax bill was $10k which he paid in the following March and was able to keep the excess tax provision held. But since he lodged his tax return in August the ATO entered him into PAYG instalments. So, from the September quarter, and then December, March and June quarters he paid

PAYG, an instalment of 2500 per quarters. So, in this phase of PAYG, it feels like you are paying two years of tax in one, with both the original tax bill of $10k and then the PAYG instalments of $10k. Luckily, Bob had kept aside some tax for the first tax bill of his business and used the extra provisioning to go towards the upcoming PAYG instalments. In the subsequent years, when he does the tax return the PAYG instalments are a credit of tax paid, meaning he has probably and likely already paid most of his tax already. That tax return will reconcile extra tax to pay if his profits have gone up or refund if his profits have gone down. In this example, we have simplistically assumed he had no other income. Also note if he did his tax return later, the PAYG instalment amounts of $10k would be squeezed into the remaining quarters left for the year, so if done as late as possible, the following year, the PAYG instalment in June would be the full $10k due in July following the June.

- When the ATO has seen you have previous business profits, it makes an estimate for you and asks you to pay quarterly business tax instalments, which come off your tax payable when you do your annual tax return.

Goods and Services Tax (GST) and Registration:

Who should register for GST

- You must register for GST if:

- Your business or enterprise has a GST turnover (gross income of business activities minus GST) of $75,000 or more

- Your non-profit organisation has a GST turnover of $150,000 per year or more

- You provide taxi or limousine travel for passengers (including ride-sourcing) in exchange for a fare as part of your business, regardless of your GST turnover – this applies to both owner drivers and if you lease or rent a taxi

- You want to claim fuel tax credits for your business or enterprise.

- If your business or enterprise doesn't fit into one of the above categories, registering for GST is optional. However, if you choose to register, generally you must stay registered for at least 12 months. When you optionally choose to be GST, registered you may elect to lodge BAS returns annually.

Your GST turnover is your gross business income (not your profit), excluding any:

- GST you included in sales to your customers

- Sales that are not for payment and are not taxable

- Sales not connected with an enterprise you run

- Input-taxed sales you make

- Sales not connected with Australia.

- Does not include any non-business other income such as investment income or wages

The Implications of being GST registered…

- You must issue tax invoices and charge GST at the current rate of GST.

- You must remit the GST collected on sales less GST paid or purchases to the ATO via a BAS Business Activity Statement Return

- We suggest accounting software to help calculate and account for the GST amounts.

- We also suggest you keep aside GST amounts in a separate bank account so as not to misjudge your cashflow position.

How should you do Tax Invoices?

If a customer requires a tax invoice they are entitled to receive one. If a business does not provide one, the customer generally needs to withhold the top tax rate from the payment of the invoice to you.

If the business has applied for an ABN recently the payer may offer to hold their payment until the ABN and tax invoice can be completed.

If the payer does withhold payment it must complete a form called PAYG Payment Summary – Withholding where ABN not quoted. Found on ATO website <u>PAYG payment summary – withholding where ABN not quoted | Australian Taxation Office</u>

Obviously, no business wants to have tax withheld for not providing a tax invoice, hence this should be strictly adhered to or perhaps not commencing trading it's good and services until ABN and tax invoicing requirements can be met.

Additionally, this theory is vital to know for any business as to validly claim GST on purchase credits they need to assert and receive a tax invoice or comply with withholding tax from the payment rules.

Example 1: Tax invoice for a sale under $1,000

Tax invoice

Windows to Fit Pty Ltd
ABN: 32 123 456 789

15 Burshag Road
Festler NSW 2755

Date: 1 August 2010

To: Building Company
254 Burshag Road
Festler NSW 2755

Description of supply	Total
Window frames	$825
TOTAL PRICE INCLUDING GST	$825

Example 2: Tax invoice for a sale of more than $1,000

Tax invoice

Windows to Fit Pty Ltd
ABN: 32 123 456 789

15 Burshag Road
Festler NSW 2755

Date: 1 August 2013

To: Building Company
254 Burshag Road
Festler NSW 2755

Qty	Description of supply	Unit price	GST	Total
50	Window frames	$150	$15	$8,250
10	Deadlocks	$40	$4	$440
TOTAL AMOUNT PAYABLE				$8,690

The total price includes GST

Lodging your BAS or GST return

- You report and pay GST amounts to the ATO, and claim GST credits, by lodging a business activity statement (BAS) or an annual, quarterly or monthly GST return depending on the GST cycle you are on.

- Tax Agents can lodge your BAS, while giving you accuracy, correct lodgement, longer to lodge and pay, as well as forecasting your year-to-date GST and tax position.

- As mentioned GST registration is required if gross sales turnover exceeds $75,000 annually. This may make some businesses less competitive and effectively 10% more expensive, particularly when they are selling private goods and services to non-businesses who cannot claim the GST on their purchase.

- It is important to understand that when you are GST registered, your sales of $1100 is income of $1000 and GST needs to be paid to the government which is not yours of $100. Also, if you had GST claimable purchases of $550, $500 are expenses and $50 can be claimed back off of the GST paid.

- Therefore, simplistically, profit would be $1000 less $500, so taxable income would be $500

- In your, GST return called a Business Activity Statement (BAS), you would pay GST of $100 on sales less $50 on purchases, equalling $50.

- BAS returns may need to be lodged on a monthly, quarterly or annual cycle. Most typically on a quarterly cycle for quarters ending 30 September, 31

December, 31 March and 30 June. These are generally due on the following 28th of the following month.

- There is a special extra grace period for the December quarter for the festive season and this one can be lodged by 28th February.
- Monthly BAS returns are due on the 28th of the following month.
- Annual BAS returns are due when your income tax return is due. This is 31 October if you do not have a tax agent and are a self-lodger. Or up to May 15th of the following year if you have a tax agent and have a good lodgement history such as have non overdue tax returns. The annual cycle can only apply when you have voluntarily elected to be GST registered and your turnover must be low $75000. This may apply to business they have no GST or their sales or may have large upfront purchases and wish to claim GST on purchases.

- It is vital to lodge these on time to avoid fines and late payment interest charges. Getting behind on BAS return obligations in business can really get you into a big debt trap, so keep up to date with BAS returns.

When to charge GST and when not to:

- Some Sales are exempt from GST. For more information on this a listing is on the ATO web link provided here.
- When to charge GST (and when not to) | Australian Taxation Office

- https://www.ato.gov.au/businesses-and-organisations/gst-excise-and-indirect-taxes/gst/when-to-charge-gst-and-when-not-to/gst-free-sales
- Input-taxed sales | Australian Taxation Office

Ways to do BAS Lodgements:

- For businesses registered for GST. There are two ways to lodge either by paper or by electronic methods. Paper forms may be sent to you by mail. Electronic methods include having your tax agent lodge, by accounting software or on your online service with the ATO accessible via your ATO connection with your digital access called MyID. In general, the BAS return needs you to complete the sales turnover for the given period of the BAS return. The GST on sales less the GST on purchases. Additionally, some other amounts may be payable such as pay as you tax instalments explained earlier which is calculated for you as a fixed instalment amount or a percentage determined by the ATO times by your period sales turnover. The PAYG instalment amount adds to your BAS amount due.

- If you are registered to have employees. You also need to disclose gross wages paid for the period and wages tax paid. The wages tax paid adds to your BAS amount due.

EMPLOYMENT LAW CONSIDERATIONS

- When hiring employees, ensure compliance with some key considerations when hiring staff

- Thinking about employing staff but unsure where to start? Hiring employees is a big step for any business, and ensuring you meet all legal, financial, and administrative requirements is essential. Here's a straightforward guide to help you navigate the process.

Understanding Employment Laws

- Before hiring, it's important to familiarize yourself with:

- **Fair Work Act & National Employment Standards (NES):** Ensure compliance with employment laws, including minimum wages, leave entitlements, and termination procedures.

- **Awards & Enterprise Agreements:** Determine the applicable award or agreement for your industry to set correct pay rates and conditions.

- **Work Rights Verification:** Use the **Visa Entitlement Verification Online (VEVO)** service to check the work rights of potential employees.

Recruitment & Onboarding

- **Job Descriptions:** Clearly define roles, responsibilities, and required qualifications to attract suitable candidates.

- **Recruitment Process:** Advertise the position, screen applicants, conduct interviews, and check references.

- **Onboarding:** Provide structured training, introduce company policies, and ensure employees understand their rights and responsibilities.

Workplace Culture & Compliance

- Foster a **positive and inclusive workplace** to enhance employee satisfaction and retention.

- Ensure staff understand their **rights regarding wages, workplace safety, and entitlements**.

- Implement a **performance management system** to set goals, offer feedback, and support career growth.

Payroll & Tax Requirements

- **Payroll Setup:** Establish a system to manage wages, tax, and superannuation payments.

- **Pay As You Go (PAYG) Withholding:** Register with the ATO to withhold tax from employee wages. You are able to do so via online ATO services or ask your tax agent to do for you.

- **Superannuation Contributions:** The current minimum superannuation guarantee rate is **12%** of an employee's ordinary earnings. Past and future amounts are available on the ATO web link Super guarantee | Australian Taxation Office.

- **Record Keeping:** Maintain accurate payroll records, including tax withholdings and super contributions, for at least five to seven years (for companies).

- **Single Touch Payroll (STP):** Report payroll data directly to the ATO with each pay run. This is done on ATO-compliant accounting software.

- **Work Cover Insurance:** Required for all employees to cover work-related injuries (e.g., **ReturnToWorkSA** in South Australia).

- **Tax File Number (TFN) Declarations:** Collect and lodge TFN forms with the ATO.

- **Fringe Benefits Tax (FBT):** If you provide benefits such as a company car, ensure compliance with FBT regulations. Generally, this will not apply to small business but for more information https://www.ato.gov.au/businesses-and-organisations/hiring-and-paying-your-workers/fringe-benefits-tax

Privacy & Employee Data Protection

- The **Privacy Act 1988** and **Fair Work Act** outline employer responsibilities regarding employee data.

- **Employee Records Exemption:** Personal employment records are generally exempt from the **Australian Privacy Principles (APPs)** if used solely for employment purposes.

- Employers must **protect sensitive employee information**, including health and tax records.

- Employees have the **right to access and correct their personal information**.

Ensuring Correct Wages & Entitlements

- To pay staff correctly:

- Check **minimum wage rates** (as of **July 1, 2024**, the National Minimum Wage is **$24.10 per hour** or **$915.90 per week** for a 38-hour week).

- Use the **Fair Work Pay and Conditions Tool** to determine correct pay, including penalties and allowances.

- Conduct **regular payroll audits** to ensure compliance with wage laws.

- Stay updated on **Fair Work Commission** decisions affecting minimum wages and awards.

- **Final Tip: Seek Professional Support**

- **Need more information?** Visit the ATO's **Hiring Employees** page or learn about **Single Touch Payroll**.

- Current regulations require you to set up Payroll and pay employees in a system called Single Touch Payroll. This effectively sends all employees' pay information to the Australian Tax Office (ATO) at each payday or pay run. This increases the integrity of the tax system by giving ATO live and current pay information throughout the year, ensuring taxes from wages, and superannuation payments, compliance is more easily monitored and policed. Generally, it is recommended that online software is used enabled with single-touch payroll capability, when a business intends to hire employees. There is no manual way to pay employees anymore.

FINANCIAL MANAGEMENT TIPS & TAX OBLIGATIONS

Tracking Your Scoreboard

Understanding your financial position is critical especially in the early stages of a business. Focus on:

- **Cash Flow:** Monitor inflows and outflows to avoid shortages.

- **Budgeting:** Plan expenses to ensure stability.

- **Pricing Strategies:** Set competitive yet profitable prices.

- **Knowing your profit or loss:** This is so you know if you are winning or losing, keep you on track, set your pricing and budget for taxes. Not knowing how your business is going, is like flying blind. By knowing how your business profits are tracking will help you feel in control of the business, not feeling overwhelmed and understanding your numbers as a proof that you are on the winning track can make your business feel even more enjoyable.

- **Here are some templates to use if not using accounting software:** business income and expenses by Romeo Caporaso pdf PDF version, print, and write on it business income and expenses by Romeo Caporaso Xls version spreadsheet.

Tax Planning

- Set aside 30% of profits for tax provisions and 10% GST payable amounts of Sales (when GST registered).

- Use accounting software (e.g., Xero, MYOB, Reckon and QuickBooks) for efficient tax reporting. This software, are a fully integrated accounting systems, they are well designed with many features to make your accounting easier and simpler to comply with. This is recommended when you are GST registered and/or pay employees.

GST Registration

Businesses must register for GST if:

- Annual sales turnover exceeds $75,000.

- Non-Profit organisations if sales exceed $150,000 turnover.

- Taxi/rideshare services are offered (regardless of income).

- Fuel tax credits are claimed.

Registration must be completed within 21 days of exceeding the threshold to avoid penalties.

What happens if your business makes a loss?

Generally, for sole trader business operators, business losses cannot offset other taxable income but must be carried forward to offset against future profits of the business. However, there are some exceptions the most common is that, if your business income is above $20,000, you may immediately offset losses against other income. This may apply, if you are operating a business and continuing to receive other income such as investment income or wages.

Separate bank accounts for your business

Having a separate bank account for your business establishes a proper framework to capture all income and expenses of your business.

Conversely, paying for expenses in various personal bank accounts is likely to make you miss claiming expenses as you may be hiding them by haphazard spending from bank accounts.

Using separate business bank accounts from personal accounts makes it easy to capture all transactions from each line of your bank statements or by connecting a bank feed to your online accounting software.

Importantly, in the case of an ATO audit, you will appear more professional in conducting your business in business bank accounts. You will be able to provide them with bank account statements showing only business-related transactions and avoid showing them unnecessary personal transactions such as food shopping, or school fees.

What about my superannuation when I am in Business?

When you are self-employed and in business, typically, as a sole trader, you will not pay an official wage as per single touch payroll, but rather simply draw funds to live on from your business profits, called drawings. Of course, if you wish to make yourself an employee of your own business you can too. This may be a way of regulating your wages, taxes being paid, superannuation being paid and worker's insurances being paid, but this must be done by single touch payroll as previously explained.

Contributions to superannuation are voluntary to a self-employed person when not an employee and are a tax deduction, but you must complete a form called Notice of intention to claim super contribution it can be found here notice in the approved form. There is a current limit on this deduction of $30k per year, more about concessional (before-tax) contributions cap and unused limit may be carried forward too,. If your income is over $250k, there may be an extra tax on your contributions of 15% called Division 293 tax. If you exceed your superannuation contribution cap, you will have to pay extra tax, and any excess concessional contributions you leave in super will count towards your non-concessional contributions cap.

As mentioned, superannuation contributions are voluntary when you are not paying yourself a wage. In this circumstance, I typically recommend that to make contributions to superannuation when your profit is above $80000. Below this amount, my view is that your cash flow is too low to afford the superannuation contribution. Remembering that superannuation contributions are not generally withdrawable until retirement.

If your income is below $47488 and you make personal non-concessional (after-tax) contributions to your super fund, the government may also make a co-contribution up to a maximum of $500. In this case, you do not claim it as a tax deduction to receive the super co contribution.

The government co-contribution you receive depends on your income and how much you contribute. Government contributions | Australian Taxation Office

You don't need to apply for the super co-contribution. When you lodge your tax return, the ATO will work out if you're eligible. If your super fund has your tax file number (TFN), they will pay it to your super account automatically.

MARKETING STRATEGIES FOR NEW BUSINESSES

Goal number one of a business is to achieve its first sale or revenue. I recommend more than one marketing strategy to gain more overall sales success. Some common approaches are outlined here.

Cost-Effective Marketing Approaches

Strategy	Description
Social Media Engagement	Use platforms like Facebook, Instagram, and LinkedIn for brand visibility.
Email Campaigns	Build an email list for promotions and updates.
Local SEO Optimization	Register on Google My Business and use location-based keywords.
Networking	Attend local events, sponsorships, and collaborations.
Free Samples/Branded Swag	Encourage word-of-mouth marketing.
Structured Marketing Plan	Define audience demographics and outreach methods.
Google your business page and other web listings	An easy way to rank well in search engines that ca drive sales leads to you

PROTECTING BUSINESS & PERSONAL ASSETS

Strategies for Asset Protection

- Choose a Pty Ltd company for limited liability.

- Use separate entities (e.g., trusts) for valuable assets. Keeping investment Assets away from business risk and trading entities.

- Secure comprehensive insurance coverage (e.g., public liability, professional indemnity).

- Avoid personal guarantees on loans and contracts.

- Ensure clear contracts and legal agreements to prevent disputes. Particularly when having other partners in your business such as a partner in a partnership. Legal documents such as a partnership agreement, can mitigate the risks and clearly define situations such as profit sharing or business exit situations which can commonly cause legal litigation.

- Have any contracts and engagement letters with customers prepared by them or service agreements checked by your lawyers for scary clauses such as indemnification clauses.

<u>Mandatory & Recommended Insurance Coverage</u>

Insurance Type	Mandatory?	Applies To
Workers Compensation	Yes	Employers
Compulsory Third Party (CTP)	Yes	Businesses with vehicles
Public Liability	Industry-based	Certain occupations
Professional Indemnity	Industry-based	Service providers
Business Property	No	Recommended for all businesses
Product Liability	No	Recommended for suppliers

For further advice, most businesses seek the advice and recommendations of insurance companies or brokers.

GOVERNMENT GRANTS & BUSINESS RESOURCES

Grants frequently change so we recommend you doing your own research. Some guidance is given here.

Available Grants

Grant Type	Description
Startup Business Grants	Varies by state; supports new businesses.
Innovation Grants	Accelerating Commercialisation program.
Wage Subsidies	Up to $10,000 for new hires. Wage subsidies - Department of Employment and Workplace Relations, Australian Government
Instant Asset Write-Off	Allows deductions for asset purchases. Check on the latest laws via your accountant or ATO website

Key Resources

- **Business.gov.au:** Government support, grants, and compliance information.

- **ATO Guidelines:** Tax and GST compliance details.

- **Small Business Advisory Services:** Free or subsidized startup consultations.

WHY USING ONLINE ACCOUNTING SOFTWARE SUCH AS XERO?

Xero, the popular cloud-based accounting software, has introduced several new updates designed to enhance the user experience for small businesses and accountants alike. Here's a look at some of the latest features that can streamline accounting tasks and boost efficiency:

Improved Bank Reconciliation

The new bank reconciliation feature now offers smarter matching capabilities, allowing users to reconcile transactions with greater accuracy and speed. This feature helps ensure that bank statements are aligned with business transactions, reducing manual entry and the risk of errors.

Enhanced Reporting Tools

Xero has revamped its reporting tools, making it easier for businesses to generate insightful financial reports. Users can now customise reports with more flexibility, add annotations, and share these reports with stakeholders directly within the platform. This is particularly useful for tax time, as detailed, organised reports are essential for accurate filings.

Multi-Factor Authentication (MFA) Update

To improve security, Xero has enhanced its Multi-Factor Authentication process, ensuring that user accounts are more secure from unauthorised access. This update is crucial for protecting sensitive financial data in an increasingly digital landscape.

Automated Invoice Reminders

Xero's automated invoice reminder feature has been fine-tuned to give users greater control. Businesses can now set customised reminder schedules based on the customer's payment history, ensuring more timely payments without manually chasing invoices.

New Projects Feature Enhancements

The "Projects" feature, designed for tracking time and costs on jobs, has seen updates to its budgeting and cost-tracking functions. These updates make it easier for businesses, particularly in service industries, to track profitability on a project-by-project basis and ensure that all costs are accounted for.

Integration with Payment Services

Xero now offers even more integrations with online payment platforms, making it easier for businesses to get paid faster. With integrations like Stripe and PayPal, customers can pay invoices directly through Xero, helping improve cash flow for businesses. Stripe can also accept payment with integration into invoices sent by email by clicking the payment processing button. Alternatively, Stripe now accepts payments by customers tapping with your devices that have Google, or Apple Pay cards enabled.

Mobile App Improvements

The Xero mobile app has also seen updates, with a more user-friendly interface and new functionalities. Users can now reconcile accounts, send invoices, and track expenses with greater ease from their smartphones, making it easier to manage finances on the go.

These updates highlight Xero's commitment to making accounting simpler, more secure, and more efficient for small businesses. By using the latest features, businesses can save time, reduce errors, and focus on growth.

Common online accounting software to consider

Set up your accounting software from these links. I have mentioned Xero, but there are alternative software choices. They all have monthly subscription fees outlined on their websites provided below.

Pricing Plans | Xero AU
MYOB Plans & Pricing – Start Your Free Trial Today
Accounting, Business & Bookkeeping Software | Reckon AU
Best Accounting Software for New Businesses - QuickBooks

Why have online accounting software rather than manual or spreadsheet record

Although accounting software has costs, these can be well worth the investment. This is because they are highly recommended when you have these two complexities. Firstly, of GST registration and accounting software makes it easy to collate all GST payable on sales and all GST credited on all purchases, thus making it easier to comply with GST reporting. Secondly, on Wages to pay for complying with Single Touch Payroll compliance, and calculating complex calculations like tax withheld, superannuation accruals, and leave accruals/payments. Additionally, accounting software saves you time to make your bookkeeping as quick and efficient as possible. If they save you hours, they are worth it, as you can sell more and do other better things with your time. They also save you from inventing a records system, and integrate many wonderful features to assist in running your business such as invoicing, payment processing, reporting your profit statement, and forecasting cash flows. They are all just a click away on your internet browser. They make collaborating with your accountants easy for queries, and of course, to provide them the information to meet your tax compliance requirements, this is called inviting in your adviser.

I am often asked when businesses are new or fairly new, if they should do their bookkeeping in a spreadsheet, and probably not sure why using accounting software like Xero could actually be beneficial.

Yes, doing a spreadsheet may save you a bit in not having any software costs. But isn't the time you spend on developing a spreadsheet that does what you need also a cost? After all, you are probably reinventing accounting software in your spreadsheet and probably not doing as good a job as the accounting software companies that spend thousands or even millions every year on developing and maintaining such software.

A spreadsheet may take less time for your accountant to process into a tax return and even lead to a lower tax preparation fee. But on the flip side, it may mean you are making more errors, too. Not many spreadsheets reconcile back to your bank account for starters, so you may be leaving out some deductions or lack the proper framework to capture all expenditures, missing some valuable tax benefits.

Other positives in Xero accounting software

- Easy to send your invoices, allocate payments to them, send scheduled invoices, send statements, send reminder to pay messages, and link to payment processors to accept more forms of payment. I love the regular invoices you can set up, great for say a regular monthly service fee to a client, it can all be automated rather than you doing it manually in a spreadsheet.

- Doing your GST becomes more of a breeze, easier to check your BAS before processing, and easier to code the relevant GST codes, also.

- Setting up a bank feed means your transactions appear in your software complete with populated amounts, and dates. All you need to do is to point them to the right account, or allocate the payments. Furthermore, the software remembers, and learns how you have coded the same transaction in the past, and suggests you coding. The bank feed really means that you must still keep bank statements, and invoices, but not get your hands dirty with them, as much. *Updating your daily transactions should take less time than a cup of coffee. Something no one ever says about using a spreadsheet.*

- Being internet-based your accountant can easily check in on your accounting, make a suggestion, collaborate with you, or even keep you informed on how your tax position is looking this year. Of course, there is no need to bring, or even email your accountants your file at the end of the year; they can simply hop in once you give them access by email.
- There is no software updating; it is all done for you. You simply can log in anywhere in the world with the internet.
- There is no need to back up either. Let someone else worry about keeping your valuable data stored on a cloud professionally, and save some of your network, or computer space too.
- Great reports. *This is where your spreadsheets really struggle to even do a Balance Sheet.* But Xero can give you so much from regular monthly management reports, to GST reporting, Payroll reporting, and finally fully formal interim reports which can go directly to interested parties like banks. It is so important to check in on your profitability and Xero reporting makes this a click away when you have entered all your transactions.
- Bank reconciliations are all taken care of ensuring less mistakes and omissions.
- Manage your cashflow at a glance on your dashboard page see what money is coming in and out.
- Integrated payroll. No need to keep separate records as it all works within the same software.

- Manage more than one entity accounting from the same login if you have more than one business entity.
- Allow as many users as you wish to have access as delegated, from the accountant role to read-only access.
- Fairly simple to establish, and set up the software, *ease into an established, and tested software, rather than, evolving your spreadsheet.*
- Xero is becoming so sophisticated, it can mean you are one click away from BAS return, tax return, and even loan approvals directly from the software. Now that accountants who properly use this software can offer you faster and more efficient accounting services with less time wasted on mundane bookkeeping. They can more efficiently, and therefore more affordably offer these services, or give you more added value consulting elsewhere.
- *Make your accounting a hell of a lot more fun.* It makes it a breeze to keep it up to date, save you lots of time, and actually look forward to your monthly reports. So, as I always say a good business keeps a live scoreboard, and knows how well they are doing, like the footy game knows the score, and adjusts their game, so too a business should use accounting to grow their business.

What does Xero cost?

It depends on what features or subscription you need. Here are some guidelines from them here Pricing Plans | Xero AU

SUMMARY OF WHAT TO DO TO START YOUR BUSINESS

Starting a business requires smart planning, financial awareness, compliance, and effective marketing strategies. Key takeaways:

- **Check your numbers** and scoreboard at least monthly or quarterly. Have a scoreboard, just like when you are watching a sport, you need to know if you are winning or losing. Use online accounting software when the business is large enough or complex enough such as when is GST registered, or has employees.

- **Set aside a recommended at least 30% of profits for tax provisions, plus 10% for GST if GST registered.** If these eventually are too much, they can be released back into the business, or owner funds. For sole traders, it may be a good idea to keep them in loan offset accounts until, they are due to save you loan interest.

- **Choose the best entity structure** for the business for tax, and liability protection, if possible, from accounting advisers. Obtain the required ABN for the accounting entity selection. Here is where to obtain your ABN from https://abr.gov.au/For-Business,-Super-funds---Charities/Applying-for-an-ABN/. You may want to link your business to ATO online services to track your lodgements, and tax accounts. This work via an online identification system called MyID formerly, MyGOV. Linking your business to my id is outlined here, <u>Using myID for business | myID</u>.

- **Apply for your business name** if a trading name is required, At this website <u>Register a business name | ASIC</u>

- **Register for GST when required** if turnover exceeds $75,000. Comply with BAS return, tax invoicing, and annual tax return lodgements. Seek guidance from accountants, if you are unsure of how to complete your BAS/ income tax return, and for guidance on the cycle and due dates. Make sure you do not get behind as this can rapidly increase your ATO debt which can soon escalate to high levels with penalties and be difficult to repay. Compromising your business ability.

- **Open separate business bank** accounts, trade all income, and expenses of the business though these bank accounts rather than, haphazardly using personal bank accounts. Establish your accounting bookkeeping system with using a manual bookkeeping system, or online accounting system.

- **Claim all your business tax deductions,** and declare all business income. In general, your accounting systems will pick up your expenses of running the business. There are some you may need to be aware of get assistance from your tax agent on, and if unsure ask your accountant to check the eligibility of some expenditure.

<u>Business deductions | Australian Taxation Office</u> and <u>Overview of business income and deductions | Australian Taxation Office</u>

You can claim a tax deduction for most expenses you incur in carrying on your business, if they are directly related to earning your assessable income.

Types of business expenses you may be able to claim deductions for include:

- Day-to-day operating expenses.
- Purchases of products or services for your business.
- Certain capital expenses, such as the cost of depreciating assets like machinery and equipment used in your business.

The amount of your deduction and when you can claim it will depend on the type of expense (for example, certain capital expenditures are deductible over time), and whether it has any private or domestic purpose for which you must reduce your deduction. Also, some expenses are not deductible (for example, fines).

There are 3 golden rules for what the ATO accepts as a valid business deduction:

- The expense must have been for your business, available as an allowable deduction, and not for private use.

- If the expense is for a mix of business, and private use, you can only claim the portion that is used for your business.

- You must have records to prove it. Records such as receipts, or tax invoices must be kept available for audit review purposes for five years.

  You can't claim the GST component of your expenses as a deduction if you can claim it as a GST credit on your business activity statement.

Claiming Home office expenses: these include expenses that can be claimed when you operate some or all of your business form home, you can claim the business portion of expenses. These may be running expenses such as power, phone, cleaning, internet, and furniture. Occupancy expenses such as a portion of rent and loan interest. More information on this is available at the ATO here <u>Deductions for home-based business expenses | Australian Taxation Office</u>

Claiming Car Travel

You may also be able to claim costs of motor vehicle trips in your business. There are two ways to claim car expenses. Firstly, the Cent per kilometre method, and secondly the logbook method.

<u>Cents Per Kilometre Method:</u>

- Claim a set rate (e.g., 88 cents per kilometre for 2024–2025).

- Suitable for simpler claims with less frequent car use.

- o Keep a logbook of business trips, including dates, destinations, and kilometres.

Logbook Method:

- o Calculate deductions based on the percentage of business use.

- o Requires a 12-week logbook recording all trips to determine business vs personal use. The logbook percentage calculation must be done every five years.

- o Ideal for those who use their car extensively for business.

- o Your claim is based on the business-use percentage of the expenses for the car.

- o Expenses include running costs, and decline in value, but not capital costs, such as the purchase price of your car, the principal on any money borrowed to buy it, and any improvement costs.

- o To work out your business-use percentage, you need a logbook, and the odometer readings for the logbook period.

- o You need the odometer reading at start say 11000

- o You need the odometer reading at end of three months say 21000

- o So, say your total kms are 10000

o You must also write each work-related or business trip in your logbook. You should then have a total work-related, or business km total say 7000.

o Your work-related, or business kms 7000 divided by your total kms 10000 will give you your work-related or business percentage of use of the car, in this case 70%

o You can claim fuel and oil costs based on either your actual receipts or you can estimate the expenses based on odometer records that show readings from the start and the end of the period you had the car during the year at the percentage your logbook has demonstrated (e.g. 70%).

o You need written evidence for all other expenses for the car.

Our website shows you how to do your logbook by video, and a downloadable logbook template can be found here <u>The Logbook Method: How to Claim Work-Related Car Expenses</u>

- **One more time – Know your profit especially in the early stages** - Know your scoreboard, and establish a regular reporting cycle of ideally monthly, quarterly or annually so you are aware of your business performance. You should also keep aside funds as a provision for your taxes. We recommend 30% of profit and 10% for GST if your business is GST registered. Knowing your numbers should be fun and taken seriously to succeed in your business. If you are not doing this educate yourself more or seek better ways to manage your accounting such as outsourcing it to your bookkeeping or accounting partners.

- **Explore government grants, and business resources.** <u>Grants and programs finder | business.gov.au.</u>

- **Obtain the relevant industry licenses and insurances.**

- When working with partners obtain a legal document such as a partnership agreement to formalise all the business terms and conditions of your business relationship. **Seek legal advice on** service agreements and contracts with suppliers and clients.

- **We recommend, Fine tuning sales process, and engagement letters.** Get your first sale! If you can have a commercial lawyer customise your terms, and conditions of engagement in your goods, and services provided. Get good at sales no matter what you do. It is the better salesperson who does better than the technical counterpart. Get some good sales techniques and training. A good onboarding process will mean you get and keep business and keep growing.

- **Obtain a google my business page**, a vital must-have free advertising tool on google. Do it on other search engines such as Bing too. Develop other online marketing such as websites, and social media channels. Here is the google one <u>Get Listed on Google - Google Business Profile</u>. If you do no other marketing, at least do this as your first step.

- **If employing staff**, comply with payment practices, single touch payroll, pay superannuation on time, and register for wages tax at the ATO. Pay your wages tax as part of your BAS return cycle. You need to be registered with the ATO as an employer with PAYG taxes withheld from your employees' wages and remitted to the ATO on the reporting, and payment cycle mandatory from the ATO.

By following these principles, and seeking professional guidance, entrepreneurs can build a successful and sustainable venture.

ERRORS TO AVOID

- Don't get behind on your BAS returns, tax returns tax obligations and payments. This is because fines can be imposed, and interest charges levied by the ATO. You should also avoid spending tax money that is not yours. Sticking to the tax cycle will regulate your cashflow, and meet your tax payment obligations. Taxes are a major expense in your business, and need to be appropriated in the correct manner. Here is some information on the ATO failure to lodge on time fines Failure to lodge on time penalty |, and they also charge interest charges General interest charge (GIC) rates | which are no longer tax deductible. Use a tax agent to comply with your tax obligation, and profit from their experience to help you grow your business. Early advice can prevent developing wrong financial habits which can be costly to fix. Get your business off to a good start with good advice early.

- *Excessive drawings can hurt* your business growth. Being in business requires a mindset change; you no longer receive regular wages amounts. Business cashflows can vary, and therefore profit drawings need to accommodate the business profits.

- *Pay your employees the correct entitlements* referring to the relevant industry awards you are in. Comply with single touch payroll requirements, and pay correct employee superannuation amounts on time and within the correct quarterly due date. Not paying superannuation will also lead to fines called superannuation guarantee charges which, are scary wastes of money, complex to complete, and non-deductible expenses.

- *Know how your business is performing. Do not fly blind,* and not know your business performance on a regular basis, this will leave you feeling overwhelmed and unmotivated in running your business. Conversely, knowing your business numbers will give you an idea of how you are tracking, especially in the early critical stages of business, allow you to set aside enough tax provision funds, better manage your business by having the numbers, and scoreboard it needs to be managed well. Imagine a sports game without a scoreboard, how would the players and coaches know what to do. Same with a business, run it with a scoreboard.

Good luck, and enjoy your business. Keep positive, set goals, and move towards your business goals. For many, a transition into being self-employed can be life changing, fulfilling, revitalising you in your career, and for some their occupation. We hope you do this, enjoy the ride, and benefits of your own business.

READY TO BUILD YOUR BUSINESS?

Need more advice and assistance to get you there.

TAKE THE FIRST STEP

Take the first step toward a well-advised business with the team that helped hundreds of clients build businesses.

BOOK YOUR BUSINESS ADVICE STRATEGY SESSION

Book your Business Advice Session with Romeo today:

• 60-minute personalised consultation

• Review of your current business plan

• Customised business set up roadmap

• Business knowledge and Tax strategies for business owners

TAKE ACTION NOW – DON'T MISS THE OPPORTUNITY

NEW BUSINESS ADVICE SESSION

https://outlook.office.com/owa/calendar/TaxAccountingAd
elaide2@taxaccountingadelaide.com/bookings/s/UJNewN8
2wkyMBS1WT7Gxhw2

"I've helped hundreds of Australians build their small businesses like my own. Let me show you how the right tax,

FOR MORE ACCOUNTING SERVICES

Whether you are new to business or have been in business for a while and need a better accounting solution, talk to us. We are a small business specialist who wants to guide your business to optimal accounting and growth. We minimise your tax, offer business improvement services and help you save time.

Even our free no-obligation initial meeting will help your business!

The right Accountant can give your business the edge. Call 08 8337 4460 to see if we are the right partner for you.

Book in for your business to meet with me https://bit.ly/4r9beCW. More information at Business Accounting Services | Tax Accounting Adelaide or https://bit.ly/4r6h0Wb.

CONNECT WITH ME

I would love to hear from you on your new business story or if my book has helped you on your business journey.

Welcome! I'd love to stay connected. Follow me on social media and reach out anytime!

Social Media

Stay updated and engage with me on these platforms:

- **Instagram**: https://www.instagram.com/taxaccountingadelaide/#

- **Twitter**: https://x.com/taxaccountingsa

- **Facebook**: https://www.facebook.com/TaxAgentAdelaide

- **LinkedIn Business**: https://www.linkedin.com/company/tax-accounting-adelaide/

- **LinkedIn Professional**: https://www.linkedin.com/in/romeocaporaso/recent-activity/all/

- **YouTube**: https://www.youtube.com/@TaxAccountingAdelaid

- **TikTok**: https://www.tiktok.com/@taxaccountingadelaide

Contact

https://www.taxaccountingadelaide.com/.

Let's Connect

I love engaging with my community! Feel free to leave a comment, send a message, or just say hi.

I would love to hear from you if this book has helped you and your business.

DISCLAIMER:

The information provided in this book is for general informational purposes only and does not constitute financial, legal, or real estate advice. While every effort has been made to ensure accuracy, property markets, laws, and financial conditions may change over time, and individual circumstances vary. Business practices, Accounting, tax laws, and financial conditions can change quickly, and as of 2025, government incentives and tax rules continue to be updated frequently. Readers should conduct their own research and seek professional guidance from licensed experts before making any property-related decisions. It is recommended to seek your own financial and tax advice based on your individual circumstances.

Note on legislation and tax rates

Tax rates, thresholds, and legislative references in this book are current at the time of publication. Laws and regulations may change. Readers should verify information with the Australian Taxation Office (ATO) or seek independent professional advice relevant to their circumstances.